Coed Cae Claer

Helen May Williams

Published by Cinnamon Press
Office 49019, PO Box 92, Cardiff, CF11 1NB.
www.cinnamonpress.com

The right of Helen May Williams to be identified as author of this work has been asserted by her in accordance with the Copyright, Designs and Patent Act, 1988. © 2023, Helen May Williams.

ISBN 978-1-78864-139-5

British Library Cataloguing in Publication Data. A CIP record for this book can be obtained from the British Library.

All rights reserved. No part of this publication may be reproduced, stored in a retrieval system, or transmitted in any form or by any means, electronic, mechanical, photocopying, recording or otherwise without the prior written permission of the publishers. This book may not be lent, hired out, resold or otherwise disposed of by way of trade in any form of binding or cover other than that in which it is published, without the prior consent of the publishers.

Designed and typeset in Bodoni by Cinnamon Press. Cover design by Adam Craig.

Cinnamon Press is represented by Inpress Ltd.

Acknowledgements

Some of these poems have appeared in the following publications: *Blōō Outlier Journal*, *Blithe Spirit*, *Hedgerow*, *Ink Sweat & Tears*, *The British Haiku Society Members' Haibun Anthologies*, *The British Haiku Society Members' Haiku Anthologies*, *Wales Haiku Journal*. I would like to thank their editors for their encouragement and generous feedback. 'around lockdown' was facilitated by correspondence with Annie-Marie Butler, as we exchanged haiku by email during lockdowns. During lockdowns the British Haiku Society held online gatherings. These gave me camaraderie and inspiration in such strange times. As did Laura Karadog, my inspirational online Welsh teacher. She encouraged me to dig deep in *Y Geiriadur Mawr*; any mistakes with the Welsh language are however entirely mine. I wish to thank all my family for the hope and support they afforded during the pandemic. Most of all love and gratitude to my husband, Ian, without whom none of this would have been possible.

About the Author

Helen May Williams lives in South West Wales. Formerly she taught at the University of Warwick and as Helen May Dennis wrote extensively on twentieth-century fiction and poetry. She is the author of *June: a biographical novel* (Cinnamon Press 2020), *Catstrawe* (Cinnamon Press 2019) and *The Princess of Vix* (Three Drops Press 2017). Her parallel text translation of Michel Onfray's *Before Silence* is published by The High Window Press (2020). During lockdown she participated in a befriending-by-phone project, which resulted in a publication with co-authors Dominic Williams and Mel Perry: *Hold the Line* (People Speak Up 2021).

Contents

Preface	5
around lockdown	9
the bright field	12
narcissus poeticus	36
a year in haiku	38
Endnotes	40

Preface

In the Deeds to my house, it is noted that in 1937 the one and a quarter acre field across the road is to be used solely as a garden for the farmhouse. Clearly this clause got forgotten with time and change of ownership. It was used briefly as a small campsite and then as grazing pasture for sheep. With lockdown came the opportunity to create a woodland garden. First came the research. What would grow two miles from the sea and battered by the predominantly southwesterly winds off the Celtic Sea? What was it advisable not to plant in Wales anymore because of the risk of spreading diseases? What would provide a rich habitat for insects, birds and small mammals? What would be the balance between broadleaf natives, native conifers and non-native trees? What would be the layout? What was my aesthetic? How would I source one year old whips during lockdown?

The field became the site of creativity, physical exercise, and emotional wellbeing. It took two years to plan, plant and establish. It will take centuries to develop and reach maturity. The following sequences of haiku and haibun were composed during the emergence of *Coed Cae Claer*.

for the children and all the grandchildren

Coed Cae Claer

around lockdown

> meditating while meandering
> Aristotle

02/12/2020

advent
rosemary blossoms
at the back door

13/12/2020

family's little strength
guarded
for mourning

17/12/2020

still growing
on old apple tree—
mistletoe

21/12/2020

soggy cornflakes
skeletal oak leaves
sprouting acorn

05/01/2021

recycled-yoghurt-pots-bird-feeder
disappears—
flap of crow's wings

10/01/2021

frost feathers fan
bareroot trees for planting—
quaking aspen

16/01/2021

bagging mole hills
for spring seed trays—
garden centre still closed

22/01/2021
on sighting the fox for the first time since last summer

nose down by molehill
tracking scent through hedgerow—
broad daylight breakfast

24/01/2021

stepping outside
starlings chunter—
scuttle-butt gossip

14/02/2021

two crows
scavenge bird seed—
sparrows flee

19/02/2021

that moment before
father's blue ceramic pot
slips from my grasp

26/02/2021

bramble patch
palaver of blackbirds—
prunus buds plumpen

01/03/2021

tight to the house
head tilted to spy insects—
chill wind tames raven

                                                            07/03/2021

flailing hedgerow
tyres wolf the verge—
dog-eared erosion

                                                            23/03/2021

grass seeds on tyre tracks
beech saplings in hedgerows—
guerrilla gardening

                                                            28/04/2021

stars on grass
windblown
blackthorn blossom

                                                            09/07/2021

niger-seed feeder
three goldfinches perch—
lamé-coated acrobats

                                                            23/07/2021

a whole fortnight sooner
than in your childhood—
ant swarm

                                                            03/12/2021

red admiral lured
to half-moon wall-light—
advent starts

the bright field

> First lockdown.
> March-July 2020

vixen saunters over, climbs the wall, stalks fat balls hanging from the bird table. every morning she comes to see what's to eat: blackbird embryos fallen from the nest, worms, a vole burrowing in the long grass; ears pricked for the slightest rustling, her heavy tits dangling.

vixen returns with evening. she brings her cub, climbs the old ash tree. her cub plays beneath our window. she stares at me through the double glazing. her cub *cenau* capers past. its fiery pelt brushes the windowpane.

a week passes. i look out from my study window into the field across the road. not one but two cubs in the long grass.

> mae cadnöes yn y cae
> mae dau genau yn y cae
> mae cadnoaid yn y cae
>
> in the field
> vixen's two cubs frolic—
> a skulk of foxes

> the rate of COVID-19 infections is rising rapidly across the UK.
> Mid October 2020

Jim tops the grass for the final time on his ancient blue tractor. we purchase a spraycan of surveyor's white paint. we pace, squint and mark fenceposts to define the line of paths. we use a cane and line to mark an off-centre circle. Ian brings over his caterpillar made from yellow floats beachcombed at Morfa Bychan. he places it at the centre of the circle. he retrieves two green plastic garden chairs and sits them where they catch the indian-summer sun. we sip tea and regard the layout. i plant the first two dozen trees: purple-stemmed crack willows propagated from garden-border prunings, self-sown hawthorns and hazel, a sycamore uprooted from beside Moorfield's narrow path, the spare hornbeam my daughter gave me, the crabapple my eldest son bought by mistake, thinking he was donating to charity. Jim gets in touch to say they have four prunus unhappy in pots in their windswept garden, grazed by his Wiltshire horn sheep. they are the largest trees we plant while we wait for the online orders to arrive in late November.

> pacing the path—
> rows of apple trees
> my offspring might see

everyone must stay at home, with a limited set of exemptions.
Sunday 15 November 2020

Ian rummages in his workshop. squirrelled away are stacks of they-might-just-come-in-handy off-cuts. he saws them to size, dips their tops in left-over white housepaint, knocks them in the red sandstone earth, renders the field paths visible from the field gate. next he finds white tent poles from the old gazebo a Hereford neighbour gave us. when rain daggled in Montmeyan we discovered it wasn't waterproof. now the field has definition. In 1880 it was called Stephall Settlement. the field to its southwest was called Neppool. behind our house was Stephole Mountain Field. Neppool? might it be from Old English: neat's pool. there is a dew pond in that field, but now it's fenced off to stop the cattle getting to it. or is it from *Nepeta*, cat mint? or new pool? or a corruption of a Welsh word? *Nepell*.

Nid nepell o fan hyn . . . not far from here lies a land where drivers never throw fast-food packaging onto the roadside.

> barrowing hawthorn
> pause to collect MacDonald's
> wedged in hart's-tongue fern

> PM Boris Johnson made a statement on the COVID-19 Winter Plan: the incidence of the disease is, alas, still widespread.
> Saturday 28 November 2020

there are different planting methods, depending on soil type and inclination. the simple slit, preferred by foresters mass planting conifer woods in pre-ploughed furrows. the T-cut for when your soil is clay with a tendency to crack when dry. pit planting, for specimen trees and anxious gardeners. for Jim's prunus, Ian takes out a deep turf. we turn each turf and shave off the top. i loosen the soil in the foot of each hole. Ian holds each tree in the hole as i crumble the square spit of deep red soil around its roots. we place the turf-top upside-down around each trunk. Ian wellies down onto the roots. we use the same method for the Welsh native apple, plum and damson trees. the soil is devonian old red sandstone. it isn't clay, nor is it friable. it promises succour to saplings bent by the southwesterly gales. it reminds me of childhood holidays. my father gardened on Southport sand. his grandfathers were farm labourers, tilling the Devon earth. 'poor men' according to the hearth tax returns. each Easter we drove from Southport to Torquay to stay a week with the family. we left at dawn; by mid afternoon we drove past sloping, freshly ploughed, potato fields.

out the car back window i wondered anew at the rich, gleaming red of the soil.

> across the water
> ancestors lie buried
> at St Nectan's

i get an email saying the main tree orders will arrive in December, spaced a fortnight apart. when we drove through the Queensway tunnel (the eighth wonder of the world), i comforted my teddy and my dolls, who sat in a row on the back seat beside me. teddy felt it most; i picked her up and cuddled her till we felt the slight upward incline and discerned the daylight ahead. we always stopped for breakfast in the same Wirral roadside café. one year my favourite dolly got left behind. i had abandoned her. a week later on the return journey, my father pulled up on the verge across the road, got out and marched across the A-road. a few minutes later, he emerged from the café carrying my doll in his arms.

> first frost in our field
> sun sets on prunus branch
> variety unknown

this afternoon it's mizzling; a late autumn, eiderdown duvet day. i walk in the field anyway. past the purple crackwillow. a month after planting, one leans at a 90 degrees angle on the southwest/northeast axis. i've stopped trying to right it. as i circle the field boundary, past the dying ash tree and the tiny hazel seedling by the narrow entrance to the strip of land set aside for natural regeneration, daylight slips below the neighbouring farm's wind turbine, below its high earth mound. we are perplexed; why was so much heavy machinery hired to shift such quantities of earth? was it just to dig a huge slurry pit, or do they still plan a circular milking shed? the french have a phrase for this time of day when the light dims: *entre chien et loup*, meaning dawn or dusk. in use in the eleventh century, it refers to the time of day when a man can no longer distinguish between dog and wolf because the light is too poor. mistakenly, i thought it might connote the start of spring, like lion and lamb.

> beyond the fence posts
> wolf lurks on periphery
> lambs frisk centre field

i recollect late May, when it rained from a clear blue sky. the english have a phrase for that too. apt, given that foxes dwell in that fenced-off strip of brambles, holly, ivy, dying ash, moss, lichen, bracken, fern, hazel, goat's willow, blackthorn, bluebells and foxgloves. between barbed wire fence and barbed wire fence.

>   ash branch breaks
>   fox's wedding
>   sliver moon

in the mid fifties my father took the Queen Elizabeth to New York and travelled the States. it was a business trip to see how US mail order used computers. my mother guessed he visited the fiancée who had travelled home during the war years. when he returned he brought me a blue-eyed, flaxen haired doll. she wore a pink dress with a translucent lace pinnie, black velvet shoes and a Panama hat with pink ribbons. she was bigger and better than any doll i knew.

>   dusty eyes
>   frayed pinnie
>   tacit memories

> Welsh ministers agreed that strengthened restrictions were
> necessary in Wales in the period leading up to Christmas.
> Friday 4 December 2020

i learn a new phrase: *ers lawer dydd* / a long time ago. . . a different time, a different country. sitting in the SCR over lunch, Hermione Lee asks us what journals to read; she's eager to know what's important. i say *The Ecologist*. my husband puts me down with a scathing remark; she doesn't mean *The Ecologist*, she means literary journals, like *Stand* for example. *How can i be so dumb?*

ers lawer dydd . . . . i invite Hermione to talk to my students about Willa Cather. after the talk she says, *You're different now. You were always so subdued. What happened?*

> lying on the sofa
> staring at the still life
> a tear streaks the apple

> The vaccine will start to be rolled out across Wales
> from next week.
> Saturday 26 December 2020

i take the wood ash over to the field and scatter it around the base of wild crab apple and Sweet Morgan. in the lee of the old hedgerow the ashes fall to the red earth. then i walk round and round the field. in each part the wind moves differently across the ground. it's strongest where i thought to plant filberts and cariad cherry.

> brambles scramble
> through blackthorn and goat's willow—
> nitrogen overload

For the week of 27 December 2020 to 02 January 2021
it is estimated that an average of 1.45% of the
community population had COVID-19.
Sunday 27 December 2020

overnight Storm Bella. we tread through supersaturated pasture, past the overflowing slurry pit. at the bottom of his drive Roy fishes broken boughs from the stream before it disappears into the underground cave. if it blocks and floods, the water supply will be contaminated. further on water courses down the track to Morfa frothing and foaming into the culvert.

    wind pruned dying ash
    ivy toppled blackthorn
    noon day sun breaks clouds

> The new strain of the virus is far more prevalent. This variant is far easier to spread to those that we are in close contact with, and we are seeing whole households being infected because it transmits so easily.
> Tuesday 19 January 2021

Nid nepell o fan hyn . . . Storm Christoph approaches. the rain outside the windows is horizontal. wind in the kitchen airvent sounds like jetplanes just over the next hill. there's a huge puddle outside the front door and another where Ian plans to dig a wildlife pond this spring.

i finally open your beautiful presents. when i do, i cry. they are so pretty, all hand made from natural or recycled materials. gifts: a constant reminder of the giver until we can meet again.

i walk round the field despite the low cloud, wind and fine rain. five hundred saplings suck up moisture from saturated ground. last Sunday we met Roy fishing broken boughs from his stream again. he told me not to plant oak; they don't like the red sandstone, they prefer the clay soil nearer to the coast. i've ordered 31 common oak and 11 holm oak already. i'll take my chances.

> macramé flowerpot hanger
> swinging in the wind
> bent red alder tip

> A further £250,000 has been made available to help unpaid
> carers in Wales cope with the financial pressures of the
> coronavirus pandemic.
> Thursday 21 January 2021

Storm Christoph stalks the old ash tree   mist mingles   cloud circles   midmorning light glimmers through rain   a fox nose down by the flooded molehill   follows a scent up the grass bank and through the hedgerow   s/he tracks through the gap in the hedgerow beneath the western power pole that carries high voltage lines above the butchered ash tree

a moment late s/he reappears by the old hawthorn laden with ivy a few yards to the south east of the pole   s/he traces a diverticle back to the molehill   through the hedgerow gap and away over Hulin's field

>   wild privet   hawthorn
>   ivyberries   gorse   hazel—
>   broaddaylight breakfast

> Changes to regulations for supermarkets and workplaces will
> ensure people are safer when they go shopping and strengthen
> protections in the workplace.

home schooling my granddaughter on Zoom   telling stories my mother told me   telling stories my mother told my daughter   telling stories my mother wrote down when she was eighty-five   because my daughter wasn't sure she would remember them   black bombazine and gaslight   oil lamps and potato cakes

glancing out the window   rain has turned to soft snow floating through bare branches   landing on tarmac and verges   caressing daffodils ivy and tyre-flattened plastic

>   on a north-wester
>   snow quietens *coed nepell*—
>   sparrows roost early

> The launch of a bilingual COVID-19 recovery app is part of wider support on offer for people experiencing the longer term effects of coronavirus.
> Sunday 24 January 2021

our fox is rural   long snouted   foraging for worms, moles and field voles wary   sly   driven by hunger these chill short days s/he knows about fat balls   stands awhile hoping those starlings were messy feeders

> bird-table footing
> paw print in frozen mud
> vixen diverticle

> The advice given to people who are clinically extremely vulnerable (previously 'shielding') that they should no longer attend work or school outside the home is extended to 31 March 2021.
> Friday 29 January 2021

trundling rotten branches to make a woodpile in the hedgerow gap i glimpse a sapling on the path. common alder. was it lost in the reeds during planting or has it generated from a sliver of twig? at its base it has been gnawed by rodent teeth to reach the nutritious cambium. i plant it anyway. a blackthorn is uncovered under the pile of wood i am shifting. a sturdy sapling it has survived without soil for months. i plant it too.

> natural blue twine
> biodegradable tree guards—
> bamboo from China

dimanche le 31 janvier 2021

Cher Jean et chère Helain:

Aujourd'hui il fait de la neige. Nous regardons avec plaisir par la fenêtre les oiseaux du jardin : des pinsons des arbres, des chardonnerets, des moineaux domestiques, des étourneaux sansonnets, des pies bavardes, des corneilles noires, même des grands corbeaux, des troglodytes, des merles noirs, des grives musiciennes, des accenteurs mouchets, et l'oiseau nationale de Pays des Galles le milan royal, qui circule autour des prés les plus proches de la maison. Les étourneaux sansonnets nous fournissent un spectacle émouvant qui s'appelle en anglais 'a murmuration' ; il prend lieu presque chaque soir entre chien et loup avant qu'ils se mettent à l'abris pour la nuit.

Mais à vrai dire, nous préférions tous nous deux être comme les oiseaux migrateurs que quittent notre pays vers l'approche d'hiver afin de séjourner aux climats plus doux encore que notre petit coin tempéré des îles britanniques. Nous rêvons d'être encore une fois assis tous les deux sur en banc au sommet de Mont Boron en regardant la Baie des Anges, les nageurs intrépides, les flottes de petits canots, les avions qui arrivent à l'heure exacte chaque après-midi, etc. etc. Tous cela nous manque terriblement.

Heureusement qu'il y a de l'espoir maintenant ; le vaccin, même les vaccins arrivent. Alors nous espérons à reprendre haleine au sommet de Mont Boron d'ici un ans!

En contre temps nous vous prions d'accepter l'expression de nos salutations distinguées, et surtout restez en sécurité et en bonne santé,

> I place dogfood in
> that hedgerow gap—
> fox prints in snow

> The introduction of an enhanced Covid-19 testing programme for care homes, which includes the twice-weekly testing of asymptomatic care home staff using rapid lateral flow test devices in addition to the weekly PCR test that is currently carried out.
> Friday 5 February 2021

we finish the planting before lunch. In the afternoon we have a cup of tea then drive down to Meddygfa Taf for our first dose of the Oxford AstraZeneca Covid 19 vaccination. we eat a whole bag of Tesco's finest crisps between us and drink Aldi's Toro Loco organic red wine in celebration. we sleep in separate beds to be on the safe side.

> alphabet of trees
> hedgerows   tall grasses   fireweed —
> spells drawn from earth

> Schools are still expected to provide education for vulnerable children and children of critical workers, and special schools and pupil referral units should continue to remain open.
> Saturday 6 February 2021

in the morning we compare notes on our broken night's sleep. Neither of us feels very clever. Annie emails me: 'Educate me sometimes about the use of a pronoun in haiku? Okay in the westernised versions?'

Depends whom you ask. Technically if you're anything approaching a purist, the haiku should remain impersonal. But I'm of the view that we have more rules about haiku in the West than the Japanese do, and that Basho wrote about himself all the time. I suppose a *Blithe Spirit* or British Haiku Society editor might want to change my haiku to:

> dogfood placed in
> that hedgerow gap—
> fox prints in snow

or

> fox prints in snow—
> dog food put out
> in the hedgerow

If I send stuff off for publication, I sometimes remember to knock out the personal pronoun and work round it with a different part of the verb (here it's the past participle but sometimes the present particle works well). Then of course I come up against my belief that it's good to have strong, active verb forms in poetry, since it gets more energy into the poem.

Then again, towards the end of his life in his 'late style' Basho favoured haiku without any verbs whatsoever. He thought that if you used nouns instead, the effect was of 'lightness'. Which he was aiming for then.

Then again, again, when he was a young man, he loved wordplay and puns.

I guess we better just do the best we can on any given day and not get too hung up about it.

> dying ash trees
> sculpt dark hieroglyphs
> send wood wide web texts

> A phased return to face to face learning for 3–7 year olds will begin from 22 February 2021.
> Tuesday 9 February 2021

i wake to predawn   open the blackout curtains   three crows are perched on the topmost tipmost branches of the dead ash that stands too close to the Western Power overhead cables   sunlight catches the spiral tree guards   they stand sentinel on frozen turf

a quarter of a century ago ... *ers lawer dydd*   three Navajos told me what i already knew from books   how they rose to greet the dawn each day   kneeling to the rising sun as he emerged above the horizon   how their womenfolk divorced them by setting their belongings outside the front door to the Hogan   this said with a self-depreciating chuckle   *had it happened to them already*

the eastern horizon is flushed pink   the morning sky is washed pale blue   golden yellow tints emerge   the crows watch patiently   it's as if they chose the tallest tree crown to see beyond the horizon

the Navajo call themselves *Diné* 'The People'   the Welsh for 'man' is *dyn*   Ket kindred across millennia and thousands of miles

> three crows
> worship its red glow—
> matins

> On 12 April all children and students will return to face-to-face education in Wales, all non-essential retail will be able to reopen, and travel will be allowed out of Wales into the rest of the UK, the Channel Islands, the Isle of Man and the Republic of Ireland. Welsh Ministers are aiming to reopen outdoor attractions and outdoor hospitality including cafes, pubs and restaurants on 26 April.
> Saturday 27 March 2021

spring begins

i wake as the dawn slips over the top of the blackout curtains i draw the curtains   look across to where seven hundred recycled plastic tree guards glint in the horizontal light of the just risen sun

> Lundy & Caldey
> float on marine light
> upturned coracle halos

later i shall circle three times around the field   peer into each tree guard to find the first unfurling

> Ynys Wair ac Ynys Bŷr
> golau mar arnofiol
> cwryglau corongylch

Saturday 7 August 2021

yesterday my sons came to visit me, to see for themselves how i am after my TIA. i walk them down to Morfa Bay then we drive back home for a simple lunch. i encourage them to finish the cheese, now that we have decided to avoid all dairy. for our health and for the health of the planet. after lunch i can see they are keen to get back on the road. it's a Friday in August; the motorway will be busy. but we walk them once round the field; show them where we want to be buried and point out the three sequoia we have just planted. Ian tells them our latest idea for the name of the wood.

he says we shall call it 'the wood of the bright field' or in Welsh—*coed cae llachar*. i say, i thought we agreed it will be *Coed Cae Claer*. i like the simplicity of this, like R.S.'s 'bright', when he could have used a loaded word. and i delight in the thought that in years to come, people might think it's connected to nearby St Clears. St Clears is *Sanclêr* in Welsh, a step nearer to the French *sanglier*, that gave it its name, when wild boar roamed the woods here. of course *cae claer* must derive ultimately from the Latin *ager clārus*.

>   rouge smudge
>   through hawthorn   hazel   blackthorn
>   dawn after dawn

mercredi le 5 janvier 2022

Chère Helene:

Ce Noel a été extrêmement difficile et triste. Jean et moi auraient dû prendre l'avion à Paris pour célébrer chez notre fils et sa famille. Mais le destin s'est décidé autrement. Jean s'est éteint le 22 décembre.

Il est tellement soudain et tellement triste.

> cherry still blossoms
> when metonymy fails

Saturday 15 January 2022

a day of blue sky   high pressure   clear sunlight in near freezing temperatures . . . we walk in the field . . . at first i only notice a few spiders' webs catching the sunlight   strung on the delicate branches of purple crack willow and young alder saplings . . . then we see they are everywhere festooning every sapling   dogwood cutting and two year old whip . . . on last summer's seed heads they make elaborate cat's cradles . . . on oak beech hornbeam and hawthorn they weave skeletal structures   incomplete nets . . . a once in a season revelation brought about by the lingering mist in the air and the bright low midday sun . . . i pray they won't snare the ladybirds hibernating in the long grass stems caught in the tree guards

> gossamer shimmer
> delirium of starlings
> first birthday boscage

Tuesday 1 March 2022

i go to plant a silver birch, but when i lift the convex dustbin lid i left lying to discourage the grass round its planting site, i discover a perfect rounded nest of dried, shredded grass stems . . . in it lies a russet field vole . . . sleepily it moves off into the long grass.

i replace the old dustbin lid and leave.

> russet field
> tread softly on the red soil
> vole dozes

> between two vapour trails
> gliding on empty
> — red kite

Tuesday 17 May 2022

rainfall resumes after the April drought. southwesterlies re-establish. walking the field i free the smaller saplings from clumps of grass caught in spiral tree guards. wishing i had held my nerve & not bought plastic.

the saplings were so tiny when they arrived. dried out & despondent from their journey in black plastic packaging. i wondered whether they were dormant or dead.

now they thrive on May warmth   clement moisture   old red devonian soil.

already some are thigh high. waist high. shoulder high. head high.

i wonder: will mother trees emerge among these assembled siblings?

> bright orange balloons
> cavort on this oak leaf
> welcome gall wasps

Wednesday 22 June 2022

i regret the tree guards. Ian erects two perching posts to encourage raptors.

a crow perches on the overhead western power post instead. a waning crescent lingers past noon. i lose count of the cocksfoot, fescues, meadow foxtail, timothy, yorkshire fog.

for days meadow browns elude me, choosing the yellow rattle and buttercups. now they move to the brambles, wild roses, dog roses, never pausing to stretch out their wings. the ash trees in the hedgerow grow robustly.

is there resilience in this field?

>   summer solstice
>   meadow browns flutter by
>   ceaseless

Friday 24 June 2022

i perceive as a child in this scene, seeing the carpet of bluebells — those fairy-blues, pinks, whites and glossy green — from my perch in the sycamore tree. pruning, my father has left two branches for me to clamber up. i watch the blackbird's nest in the ivy that clings to the impregnable bottom wall. i see the black ants tending the greenfly and trailing milk back to their nursery.

    the scent of compost
    the stickiness of aphids
    field memory

recovering from measles i cut out the flower fairies and pasted them in my scrapbook. YaYa polished the silver and dusted the bedrooms, her flowered apron strapped tight round her bosom. she stayed with me when my mother caught the bus to town, stooping to straighten her seams before donning her leather gloves even in spring.

    dart across the path
    somersault in the ash branch
    the wren

Thursday 14 July 2022

outside my window the combine harvester backs bleeping to let the tourist car through. round the bend. the council have cut the verges. immature seedheads mown under midsummer sun. mexican fleabane has self-seeded between the pavers on the yard. borage lovage ragged robin cow parsley rosebay willowherb pineapple weed pale willowherb herb robert self heal meadow buttercup creeping buttercup dandelion daisy oxeye daisy musk mallow evening primrose yellow vetch purple vetch red campion white campion forget me not red clover white clover opium poppy teasel knapweed knautia widow flower meadow cranesbill cornflower hairy willow herb burdock plantain comfrey fox and cubs marigold granny's bonnet silver weed white musk mallow yarrow . . . i lose track

    found poem
    garden weed
    found wild flower

my parents' wedding anniversary.
Wednesday 17 August 2022

we get the letter saying there will be a hosepipe ban   the water butts are low   i save the precious rain water for the blueberries   we wait for the cool of the evening before we walk in the field   a chestnut cat is hunting   intent on the long grass beside the regeneration strip   she doesn't move as we approach   she eyes us coolly and returns to her vigil

the following evening i water the plants i've just planted in the bog garden i dug   she is hunting in the garden this evening where we have left the grass to grow all summer   she approaches wary yet anxious to befriend

we chat a little   then two kittens creep towards us from the dutch barn   creep then run back   creep then run back   creep then settle down to listen and watch

    mae cath yn y coed cae claer
    mae cath ac dai gath fach
    yn y arth

we feed them the dry dogfood we bought for the fox.

narcissus poeticus

yearling sheep shed wool
narcissus poeticus—
white bubbles on green

dawn mauves elder-flower
blackbird thumps window
magpies feast

barberry shelter . . . purple willow . . .
llygad llo Mawrth . . . blodyn neidr

my avatar tends
attar of rose   geraniums
night-scented stock

hydrangea sweetness
tea of heaven
thrives on neglect

in sunlight   share
glistening blackberries
with bluebottles

clearing timothy
beneath oak saplings
smir becomes letty

on the fruitladen
triploid Jonagold
a pink bud unfurls

milky blue morning
swallows are gathering
on the wire—already

pale sun washes strand
one sea-smoothed pebble
dwells on your hearth

a year in haiku

sunrays crack horizon
rain glaciates tree trunks
tyres spray fox

dew jewels grass seed
rabbit trembles under net—
strawberry breakfast

the one shrew
skitters to ash-tree knoll
the other dithers

pubertal robin
rocks precarious stem
beaks red fescue seed

two collared doves
perch on roof ridge
passion spent this year

harvest moon sinks
on hearth's coving
a pipistrelle sleeps

fox scat
fresh
on turf

Endnotes

'the bright field' (7 August 2021) explains why we named the field *Coed Cae Claer*. For disconcerted Welsh speakers, I acknowledge that it would be more usual to call it *Coed Cae Disglair*. I couldn't resist the alliteration.

— (27 March 2021) Lundy's Welsh name refers to the wizard Gwydion, whose name means 'born of trees'. Caldey (Welsh: Ynys Bŷr) has been inhabited since the Neolithic era. A Celtic Monastery was established on the island in the sixth century. Just after the Easter following my mother's passing, I went on a retreat there.

'*narcissus poeticus*' uses two dialect words for rain, one from Scotland and one from Somerset: 'smir' is used to describe a fine, drifting rain or drizzle, 'letty' describes the sort of rain that makes outdoor work difficult.

Lightning Source UK Ltd.
Milton Keynes UK
UKHW012049210223
417406UK00005B/390